POEMS TO LIVE BY

DOG OF BLUE

Poems To Live By;
Dog Of Blue
Copyright 2017
Charles Elwell
Deborah Lee Davis

Cover design by :
Brian McDermott
mcdermott.photo.graphic@gmail.com

All Scripture, unless otherwise noted, is from the King James Version.

Published by Davis Mission
PO Box 215
Olean, NY 14760

POEMS TO LIVE BY

Many years ago my dad started writing poetry. Some of these poems he put to music. Others have been collected in small pamphlets, stored in computer memory or laying around on 3 by 5 cards. One day my dad said that he and I should make a devotional book out of his poems. So this is the first of these devotionals. At the end of each "day" I have added an open ended prayer. These prayers are designed to help you get started but they are in no way complete. Please finish each prayer time in your own words, look up more scriptures to meditate on, and develop a prayer life of your own. I believe you will be blessed and inspired each day as you read "Poems To Live By."

TABLE OF CONTENTS

TABLE OF CONTENTS

POEMS TO LIVE BY

Day 1

DOG OF BLUE

Once I had a dog of blue, Listen close the story is for you
When the sun went down, He'd lift his head
And let out a howl, That would raise the dead
Only one thing, He had on his mind
To get to the fields, A fresh track to find
And letting him out, At the edge of the wood
He'd get you one going, As quick as he could
Filling the night, With his beautiful bawl
To tree that coon, He'd give you his all
Tho tempted by deer, His path often crossed
The track of that coon, He never once lost
But kept pressing on, over river and dale
Undaunted by obstacles, He'd not give up the trail
Tired and weary, and his feet start to bleed
He'd keep pressing on, Till the coon he had treed
And if it took you till dawn, To get to the tree
When you finally arrived, There he would be
And none can deny, You may mark my word sir
He was a Sticker a Stayer
And an All Night Tree Barker

POEMS TO LIVE BY

Now he didn't know how, To shake your hand
Play with a ball, Or guard your land
Couldn't drive the cows, Or pull a sled
And his pedigree at a dog show,
He had never heard read
But to that which he'd been born and trained
He'd gladly give his life, And never complain

Now wouldn't it be great, If we all could be true
To that which we've been called,
Like my old dog of blue

Instead we think, We can do it all
From being a Bishop, To playing pro ball
And when we fail, And run a-muck
We console ourselves, And blame it on luck
But luck has nothing, To do with success
Failure is caused, By poor judgment and laziness
And temptation, Has caused many to fail
When they left the course, In pursuit of some Quail

So make your calling, And election sure
Press onto the course, Without a trace of demure
Press on press on, Tho dark be the night
Press on press on, Till broad day light
And stay at the tree, Like my ol blue hound
For when the Master comes,
That's the place to be found
Do what you do best, And try a little harder

That it may be said of you

He's a; Sticker a Stayer, and an All Night Tree Barker

ᏭᏭᏭᏭᏭᏭᏭᏭᏭᏭᏭᏭᏭᏭᏭ

Galatians 6:9
And let us not be weary in well doing: for in due season we shall reap, if we faint not.

Hebrews 11:6
But without faith it is impossible to please him: for he that cometh to God must believe that he is, and that he is a rewarder of them that diligently seek him.

Proverbs 20:4
The sluggard will not plow by reason of the cold; therefore shall he beg in harvest, and have nothing.

ᏭᏭᏭᏭᏭᏭᏭᏭᏭᏭᏭᏭᏭᏭᏭ

When I was a little girl, I heard story after story of my dad's hunting experiences. "Coon" hunting was his passion and just about every night he would hope for the perfect night to chase after a raccoon and run through a swamp following after his "coon" hounds. The best hound dog was the one who would find a particularly fat raccoon, chase the coon till he ran up a tree, and stayed at the bottom of the tree barking until my dad could catch up. This poem has always been a favorite of everyone who is a lover of his poems.

It is the nature of God to persist even when we would give up. He has called us to be like him. However in our earthly nature, we have the tendency to give up when things get tough. Take some time today to ponder on Galatians 6:9. There is a blessings for those who can endure a little more longer, try again, and not give up. The hound dog in this poem reminds me of the time that Jesus taught about prayer. He said we should ask and keep asking, knock and keep knocking, and to seek and keep seeking. This is a powerful message. Quitting is the easy way out while staying the course takes extra effort. The reward goes to the one who doesn't give up.

༄ༀ༄ༀ༄ༀ༄ༀ༄ༀ༄ༀ༄ༀ༄ༀ༄ༀ༄ༀ༄ༀ༄ༀ༄ༀ

Prayer
Father God, help me to be faithful like the "ol blue hound."
Give me the strength to finish my course. I need your help
Lord. My family, marriage, finances, need you. I know I
have asked before but here I am again. I won't give up! I'm
going to be a Sticker, a Stayer and an All Night Tree
Barker.

༄ༀ༄ༀ༄ༀ༄ༀ༄ༀ༄ༀ༄ༀ༄ༀ༄ༀ༄ༀ༄ༀ༄ༀ༄ༀ

Notes:

_____
_____
_____
_____
_____
_____
_____
_____
_____

ഇൗഇൗഇൗഇൗഇൗഇൗഇൗഇൗഇൗഇൗഇൗ

Prayer Requests

_____

_____

_____

_____

_____

_____

_____

_____

Day 2

STYROFOAM CUP

A Styrofoam cup on a window sill sat
Inside the seed - with earth firmly packed.
At last it sprouted and - with moisture and sun
The life of the flower had begun.
It grew and grew - till one day in May
To the garden it went
And the Cup?   Oh, we threw the cup away.

This treasure we hold - in jars of clay
Only for a season - we're not here to stay.
To heaven we'll be - transplanted someday
And the jar ?
Oh, the jar - they'll throw that away.

For the treasure is not - a cup of Styrofoam
Nor is it - a jar of flesh and bone.
Oh, the real treasure is - the Life of Christ within
That the praise may not be of the Vessel,
But of Him

ഽൟഽൟഽൟഽൟഽൟഽൟഽൟഽൟ

2 Corinthians 4:7-9, 4:15-18

But we have this treasure in clay jars, so that the extraordinary power belongs to God and does not come from us. We are experiencing trouble on every side, but are not crushed; we are perplexed, but not driven to despair; we are persecuted, but not abandoned; we are knocked down, but not destroyed... For all these things are for your sake, so that the grace that is including more and more people may cause thanksgiving to increase to the glory of God. Therefore we do not despair, but even if our physical body is wearing away, our inner person is being renewed day by day. For our momentary, light suffering is producing for us an eternal weight of glory far beyond all comparison because we are not looking at what can be seen but at what cannot be seen. For what can be seen is temporary, but what cannot be seen is eternal. (New English Translation)

ഽൟഽൟഽൟഽൟഽൟഽൟഽൟഽൟ

As a little girl, I planted my share of seeds in both paper and styrofoam cups. I remember impatiently waiting for the sprout to peek out of the dirt. More than once I poked around the dirt in hopes of hurrying the seedling along. But nothing made that seed shoot out a sprout before its time. As a matter of fact I probably delayed the seed from growth because of my rooting around in the dirt.

This is the same for us. The new life of God planted deep within takes time to mature. So often we want to hurry God's process along. We dig around and find a little evidence of growth but disturbing that growth process actually retards the work being done. We get so impatient waiting. We want to serve God and feel qualified for service. We want to jump way ahead of God's process and we become frustrated when others can't see how " grown up" we are. Like the seed in the black dirt, our growth has to be developed in the darkness of our spirit. No one can see the growth, and yet it is there developing on its own timetable.

Our biggest mistake is when we begin to think that the growth is ours. When actually we are only the vessel. We have no ownership, we are dead in Christ and it is Christ who lives in us and owns the seed growing inside. Like the cup that was thrown away, our body will someday be discarded but our Spirit, that which we have given to the Lord will live forever. So have patience. Water your seed with God's word. And in faith wait, knowing that the day will come when Christ in you blossoms into maturity.

ಬಂಬಂಬಂಬಂಬಂಬಂಬಂಬಂಬಂಬಂಬಂಬಂಬಂಬಂ

Prayer
Dear Heavenly Father, give me the patience to wait while you grow in me. Help me to always remember that it is Christ who is alive in me. I have made a life exchange and I am no longer alive. My thoughts, desires, and impatience I give to you. Help me to be a life which reflects you and you alone. I'm tired of trying to be in control. I give myself and all that I am to you. I am yours.

DOG OF BLUE

ഇ0ഇ0ഇ0ഇ0ഇ0ഇ0ഇ0ഇ0ഇ0ഇ0ഇ0ഇ0ഇ0ഇ0

Notes

_____

_____

_____

_____

_____

_____

_____

_____

ഇ0ഇ0ഇ0ഇ0ഇ0ഇ0ഇ0ഇ0ഇ0ഇ0ഇ0ഇ0ഇ0ഇ0

Prayer Requests

_____

_____

_____

_____

_____

_____

_____

_____

Day 3

ANYTIME YOU'RE NOT FISHING

My brother and I went fishing
Was a real nice day last May
We were trolling the reservoir when a big one hit
It was one of those big ones that got away.
We stopped for a coffee, my brother leaned back
And in his matter of fact way, He said, "Charley you know,
Anytime we're not fishing,
We're just a frittering our life away!"

Well it got me to thinking about all the things we do
To help fill out our day,
Like working hard holding down two jobs
So all the bills we can pay.
Caring for the kids, and helping the wife,
And even letting her mama come home to stay.
And you know I think brother is right.
Anytime you're not fishing,
You're just frittering your life away.

DOG OF BLUE

You can go to college,
become a lawyer, and join the N.R.A.,
Run for office, be a politician, so we all can get better pay.
Help the Guild and Ladies Aid, even attend the P.T.A..
But any time you're not fishing,
You're frittering your life away.

Now don't look at me so Holy, Hear me out!
But what is that you say?
How about going to church, paying tithes
And spending some time in prayer each day?
Or listing to Oral, Pat and Benny,
And sending them an offering, their expenses to defray
Well hold on a minute, I still declare to you,
Anytime you're not fishing, You're frittering your life away.

You see Jesus got into Peter's boat, Luke's gospel tells it,
sort-a this a-way,
The crowd was so big, out from the shore, He had to be
pushed away.
And when He got done teaching all those people
The disciples sort-a heard Him say.
"Boys let down your net for a great big catch, because,
Anytime you're not fishing,
You're frittering your life away."

Now you can give yourself to doctrine
Studying all the latest theology of the day,
Worry and fret over the music, Making sure we worship in
just the right way.

But I say get yourself an ol fishers net,
and work while its still day, because,
Anytime you're not fishing,
You're just a frittering your life away.

Jesus said, "Come unto me all you that are weary
On me your burdens you can lay".
Don't be so worried about all the problems in the church
How it's in such great disarray, Enter into His rest, be a
good witness
And take it from an old reformed type A.
Anytime, you spend, not fishing,
You're just frittering your life away

ଽଚଽଚଽଚଽଚଽଚଽଚଽଚଽଚଽଚଽଚଽଚଽଚଽଚଽଚ

Acts 1:8
But you will receive power when the Holy Spirit has
come upon you, and you will be my witnesses in
Jerusalem, and in all Judea and Samaria, and to the
farthest parts of the earth. NET

Matthew 4:18-20
And Jesus, walking by the sea of Galilee, saw two
brethren, Simon called Peter, and Andrew his brother,
casting a net into the sea: for they were fishers. And
he saith unto them, Follow me, and I will make you
fishers of men. And they straightway left their nets,
and followed him.

೮೧೮೧೮೧೮೧೮೧೮೧೮೧೮೧೮೧೮೧೮೧೮೧೮೧೮೧೮೧

The only thing we have on this earth that can never be replaced is time. This one life, is all we have ever been given. To waste our days, never giving thought to how we should invest our life is nothing short of tragic. I have heard my dad quote this poem many times, and even though I don't see myself as an "evangelist", I have spent much of my life letting people cry on my shoulder, bringing hope and peace to anyone who would listen.

How do you spend your life? A lot of time and energy is spent deciding how we will spend money but how will you spend your life? Don't live a life full of regrets. Don't waste all of your days on foolish things. At the end of your days, you will be so grateful that you spent your life investing in people for they are the only things that are eternal.

೮೧೮೧೮೧೮೧೮೧೮೧೮೧೮೧೮೧೮೧೮೧೮೧೮೧೮೧೮೧

Prayer
Father God, my life is so busy that sometimes it seems as if my days just fly by. Then all of a sudden I realize that I have not spent my time wisely. Help me to organize my life in such a way that I always have time for you. Help me not to waste my time but to invest in people. At the end of my days, I want no regrets.

೮೧೮೧೮೧೮೧೮೧೮೧೮೧೮೧೮೧೮೧೮೧೮೧೮೧೮೧೮೧

POEMS TO LIVE BY

Notes

_____
_____
_____
_____
_____
_____
_____
_____
_____

ಬಂಬಂಬಂಬಂಬಂಬಂಬಂಬಂಬಂಬಂಬಂಬಂ

Prayer Requests

_____
_____
_____
_____
_____
_____
_____

Day 4

BIRD FAITH

Like Birds they never sow or reap
But do they worry or complain, Narry a peep
For their Heavenly Father,
Has promised their Keep
We are taking Him at His word, don't you know
So why should we have, Reason to Sow
No we never sow or ever reap
For our Heavenly Father has
Promised our keep
Today is a bit too cold to plow
And harvest is such, Hard work anyhow
And what if it didn't grow ?
No ! I'll not take a chance and sow
What if I don't reap, My Heavenly Father
Has promised our keep
If you never figure on having a surplus
There is no reason for Barns or Storehouse
Just enough to meet,   Each day's need
Oh' I'll not be accused of greed
Why should I sow?

What if I don't reap?
My heavenly Father
Has promised my keep
To have bins bulging with golden grain
Would seem to them a bit too vain
What if they have no sheaves to bind?
They're happy to glean, `just what's left behind
And their brother doesn't care
If from his garden they eat

So why should they worry ? What if they `never' reap?
Their heavenly Father
Has promised their keep

Course they never have - an offering to give,
"We only, have enough on which to live"
And besides; for an offering, They never would plead
Why their heavenly father meets their need.

But although, He has promised their keep
Without sowing,
They've just enough to make ends meet.

ಐ ಐ ಐ ಐ ಐ ಐ ಐ ಐ ಐ ಐ ಐ ಐ ಐ ಐ

2 Corinthians 9:6-10
But this I say, He which soweth sparingly shall reap
also sparingly; and he which soweth bountifully shall
reap also bountifully. Every man according as he

purposeth in his heart, so let him give; not grudgingly, or of necessity: for God loveth a cheerful giver. And God is able to make all grace abound toward you; that ye, always having all sufficiency in all things, may abound to every good work: (As it is written, He hath dispersed abroad; he hath given to the poor: his righteousness remaineth for ever. Now he that ministereth seed to the sower both minister bread for your food, and multiply your seed sown, and increase the fruits of your righteousness;)

Acts 20:35
I have shewed you all things, how that so labouring ye ought to support the weak, and to remember the words of the Lord Jesus, how he said, It is more blessed to give than to receive.

Luke 6:38
Give, and it shall be given unto you; good measure, pressed down, and shaken together, and running over, shall men give into your bosom. For with the same measure that ye mete withal it shall be measured to you again.

ᏋᎣᏋᎣᏋᎣᏋᎣᏋᎣᏋᎣᏋᎣᏋᎣᏋᎣᏋᎣᏋᎣᏋᎣᏋᎣ

While it is true that the Lord has promised to keep us and provide for our every need, we know that we have some responsibility in this promise. We have to be willing to give so we can receive. In the natural it is easy to understand this. If a farmer wants to get a crop, he must give to the land some seed. So we also need to be like that farmer and sow some seed. God has promised us that when we do, there is a reward for us.

We also must guard our hearts that we don't give with a wrong attitude. How easy it is to grumble and complain while we give saying, "I had better get a good return on this investment." When we give in this attitude, we spoil our harvest. We need to be those who give with a happy heart. The scripture says that it is more blessed to give than to receive. We get a blessing when we give. It matters not what you give, you will receive a blessing. So today ask the Lord. What should I give today, a smile, a prayer, my time, or my money? Give and it shall be given unto you, pressed down, shaken together and running over!

ဆာဆာဆာဆာဆာဆာဆာဆာဆာဆာဆာဆာ

Prayer
Father, today I commit my life to you again. I want to be a giver and not a taker. Encourage my faith as I step out and sow. I give you my time and my money. I choose to be a living sacrifice.

ဆာဆာဆာဆာဆာဆာဆာဆာဆာဆာဆာဆာ

Notes

_____
_____
_____
_____
_____
_____
_____
_____

ဆာဆာဆာဆာဆာဆာဆာဆာဆာဆာဆာဆာ

Prayer Requests

_____

_____

_____

_____

_____

_____

_____

_____

Day 5

THE DUCK CHURCH

On a Sunday morn, With their best feathers on
To Church, all the ducks were gone.
Pa Pa Ducks had taken their seats,
The ducklings, were waddling around.
While all the Gals were
Straightening out their feathers
And: fluffing, up their down.
Pastor Drake was taking his text,
And had just begun to expound
While all at once, the peace was disturbed
Why someone was making a sound
A little quaker in the back, wanted to be heard
Seems he had a testimony,
About flying, like an, Eagle bird !
On the other side of the pond, it seems,
He had been, to a meeting where,
They all discovered, they could fly
And, to this he would swear.
Well they all began to quack and squawk
Everyone was in despair

DOG OF BLUE

Made enough noise to scare a hawk
The opinion of all; was, that they thought,
In scripture it could not be found
While all the gals,
Straightened their feathers
And, fluffed up their down.
Well this little fellah, Was not to be silenced;
He would not sit idly by
But: Got up, on the back of a pew, Flapped his wings
And of all things; Began to Fly !
Well he; flew right in - to, mid air
Really gave them all, a scare.
The Deacons had a meeting, and decreed
That; Flying for Ducks, there was no need.
That it; was mostly for Show
And Flying Ducks in church
The answer is, no! It should not ever be found.
While the Gals,
Straightened, their feathers
And, fluffed up their down.
Well everyone doubted, for none, had, err heard
That Ducks could fly, like an Eagle Bird.
Most were a-feared, to give it a try
But; he insisted, that they, could fly.
Well the very next thing, that I knew,
Control, was well Ny lost
They all got up, on the back of their pew,
And caution to the wind, they tossed.
Well they tossed all right, Flapping their wings,

Around and around the church they all flew.
And around the pulpit, they did fly,
Till Deacon Drake gave it a try,
And they flew and they flew around and around
Till they all tired out, and their, seats they found.
Than all the gals,
Straightened their feathers,
And fluffed up, their down.
Well everyone wanted to testify,
To make sure that everyone heard
That they had, all, really flown,
Just like an Eagle Bird
And they all agreed, from Beer-Sheba to Dan
They had never been, in a meeting so grand.
Than a closing prayer, and one more song,
The gals all,
Straightened, out their feathers,
And fluffed up their down
And they all got up, and, `WADDLED HOME.'*

* This is not original with me, I first heard it in West Africa as a funny story, I severally tampered with it and arranged it into poetry. CWE

ෂ෩ෂ෩ෂ෩ෂ෩ෂ෩ෂ෩ෂ෩ෂ෩ෂ෩ෂ෩ෂ෩ෂ෩ෂ෩ෂ෩

2 Corinthians 5:6-7
Therefore we are always full of courage, and we know that as long as we are alive here on earth we are absent from the Lord - for we live by faith, not by sight. NET

Philippians 2:12
So then, my dear friends, just as you have always obeyed, not only in my presence but even more in my absence, continue working out your salvation with awe and reverence, NET

Colossians 2:6
As ye have therefore received Christ Jesus the Lord, so walk ye in him:

ഇ ഇ ഇ ഇ ഇ ഇ ഇ ഇ ഇ ഇ ഇ ഇ ഇ ഇ ഇ

This is one of my favorite poems. I love the image of those ducks walking home after flying around the church. Sadly, I think I have done that very same thing. After a wonderful time worshiping God, feeling light hearted and unburdened only to walk out of the church and pick up those same burdens. Just like the ducks I waddled home forgetting the peace and joy, that had been so freely given.

The Apostle Paul encourages us to walk not by sight but by faith. So often we get our eyes on what is happening all around us. We see our failures and our mistakes. It is easier to pretend that we can't "fly." Blaming our situation and problems for our inability to "fly", we waddle around in defeat. Instead we can soar above this life. Keeping our eyes on the Lord and walking by faith, he can lift us out of every problem. He can lift us out of depression. He can lift us out of fear.

Today, instead of submitting to defeat, make an effort to walk by faith. Faith doesn't demand giant leaps. No! Faith walks one step at a time, keeping his eyes on Jesus. You might be surprised that you too can fly.

ᏚᏚᏚᏚᏚᏚᏚᏚᏚᏚᏚᏚᏚᏚᏚᏚ

Prayer
Father, I have been guilty of being like those ducks. I have heard your word, experienced your presence and yet I have not applied your truth to my life. Help me to be faithful to take your word with me wherever I go. Apply it to my everyday situations. As I go about my life, I want to soar with you. I don't want to spend my life waddling like a duck!

ᏚᏚᏚᏚᏚᏚᏚᏚᏚᏚᏚᏚᏚᏚᏚᏚ

Notes

_____

_____

_____

_____

_____

_____

_____

ᏚᏚᏚᏚᏚᏚᏚᏚᏚᏚᏚᏚᏚᏚᏚᏚ

Prayer Requests

_____

_____

_____

_____

_____

_____

_____

DOG OF BLUE

Day 6

BIOGRAPHY OF A BEAR

Come each fall when it gets late,
The bears and coons all hibernate
The chucks and frogs their winter to spend
Will find themselves a cozy den.
And woe to the soul, that would dare,
Go into that cave and poke that bear.
Layers of fat they will absorb,
But alas their life is exceedingly bored
And without any, appointments to keep,
They soon drift off into endless sleep.
Day and night into one do blend
As they dream of things that might have been,
Of things they would do, and trips they would take
If only they didn't hibernate.
And all the while out in the waters deep,
The beaver has an agenda to keep.
Lodges to build and dams to repair
Young'ens to train to stay out of the snare.
The fox who has no place to go
Will spend his night curled up on the snow,

DOG OF BLUE

Dawn will find him out on the trail
Listening for hounds and looking for quail.
The turkeys and squirrels in the snow filled woods,
Have left their tracks, where they've searched for food
But when it comes time for their life to close,
They could spin you a tail you could put to prose.
Of storms, and sunrises, and moons so bright
And stars that filled the skis at night,
Cutting down trees, building a dam
Making a place where the fishes swam,
Of narrow escapes from hunter and hound
And finding food on the frozen ground,
Of tales so exciting they would straighten your hair.
But its a different story, the bio of a bear.
All he can say is, he got up and ate
And went to bed with a stomach ache
Got up and ate everything he saw,
Than went to bed and waited for a thaw.
And prayed that spring would soon arrive,
That he would make it through the winter,
And come out alive.
Now when your time and work on earth is done,
And they write your name on a granite stone,
If there's room for one more line there.
Wake up and pray,
They don't write,
The Biography of a Bear.

ଛଙଛଙଛଙଛଙଛଙଛଙଛଙଛଙଛଙଛଙଛଙଛଙଛଙ

Proverbs 6:6-11
Go to the ant, you sluggard; observe its ways and be wise! It has no commander, overseer, or ruler, yet it prepares its food in the summer; it gathers at the harvest what it will eat. How long, you sluggard, will you lie there? When will you rise from your sleep? A little sleep, a little slumber, a little folding of the hands to relax, and your poverty will come like a robber, and your need like an armed man. NET

ଛଙଛଙଛଙଛଙଛଙଛଙଛଙଛଙଛଙଛଙଛଙଛଙଛଙ

Time is the only thing we can waste and never get back. Years ago people said that computers and the electronic age would come and save us all a lot of time. Oh how wrong they were. Our lives are consumed with computers and computer tech. Day after day we invest in computer games, TV shows, and gadgets galore. Why even books are no longer written just on paper with ink, but downloaded and uploaded to computers and computer banks. I have seen the time when whole days have been lost just trying to make computers work as they have been promised to do. How about you? What do you waste your time on, hobbies, extra work, reading, video games, taking care of your "stuff?" I don't want the generations that follow me to see a wasted life but a life full of the purpose of God.

Maybe you have wondered, " What is my purpose?" Spend some time alone with God. Read his word. Allow him access to your "free" time. You will be surprised at what you see and what you become. Don't let your life become "The Biography of a Bear."

಄಄಄಄಄಄಄಄಄಄಄಄಄಄಄

Prayer
Father, give me a purpose for my life. Use me. Don't let my life be remembered for my poor judgment and wasted days. I want to have an impact on my family and my community. Help me to order my days to spend more time with you. Help me to use the time I have and not lose it.

಄಄಄಄಄಄಄಄಄಄಄಄಄಄಄

Notes

_____
_____
_____
_____
_____
_____
_____

಄಄಄಄಄಄಄಄಄಄಄಄಄಄಄

Prayer Requests

_____
_____
_____
_____
_____
_____
_____

Day 7

DEAD OLD MEN

When I Was Young
I Was Told
Years Would Make
Passions Grow Cold
Youthful Temptations
I Was Told To Flee
But Where Can I Go
That, They Shall Not Be
To The Cross, I Came
A Refuge To Seek
With The Cross Applied
Temptations Retreat
I Have Been Young,
And I Have Been Old
I Have never seen
The Righteous Forsaken
Nor His Seed Begging Bread

But He Will Always Be Tempted
Until He Is Dead

Yes It's Not, "Old" Old Men
That Walk In Victory
But It's, "Dead" Old Men
That Are Temptation Free

છાછાછાછાછાછાછાછાછાછાછાછાછાછા

Galatians 2:20
"I have been crucified with Christ; and it is no longer I
who live, but Christ lives in me; and the life which I
now live in the flesh I live by faith in the Son of God,
who loved me and gave Himself up for me. NET

Matthew 26:41
Watch and pray,that ye enter not into temptation: the
spirit indeed is willing but the flesh is week.

છાછાછાછાછાછાછાછાછાછાછાછાછાછા

I think we would all like to believe that we are immune to
temptation. But temptation is all around us every day. TV,
radio and magazines produce commercials that bombard us
with things to covet and lust after. There is no end to
temptation. It is tenacious to the end, with only one goal.
That is to tempt you to buy, to have an affair, to look for a
new husband or wife, to cheat on your taxes, or cover up
wrong doing. We have every opportunity to do what is
wrong. But, if we are diligent, we can have the victory.
We don't have to be a slave to temptation. We don't have to
give in to its cravings. You see, temptations are never
satisfied. There will always be another thing to buy or lust
after. The key to victory is not to hide away but to fill your

life with the Lord. Be proactive. Read God's word. Spend time in prayer. Meditate on the goodness of God. Find a way to fight temptation before it gets a foothold on you.

℘℘℘℘℘℘℘℘℘℘℘℘℘℘℘

Prayer
Father, I have failed. There have been times when I have given in to temptation. Lord, show me the areas in my life where I am weak. Show me how to fight temptation. I want to have the victory in my life. I don't want to give in. So today, I choose to be offensive. I will fight temptation before it starts.

℘℘℘℘℘℘℘℘℘℘℘℘℘℘℘

Notes

_____
_____
_____
_____
_____
_____
_____
_____

℘℘℘℘℘℘℘℘℘℘℘℘℘℘℘

Prayer requests

_____
_____
_____
_____
_____
_____
_____
_____
_____
_____
_____

Day 8

COIN IN THE HAND OF A KING

Would you be a coin in the hand of a King?
To be spent on a slave his freedom to bring
Stamped with His image,
Inscribed with His name
To be spent as a coin someone's freedom to gain
Some one is praying to the Father today
Send some one to me to show me the way
A voice calls from heaven, Who will go for me,
To be spent as a coin, that others may be free
Would you be a coin in the hand of a king?
So many things for us to do today
Scarcely do we notice when we've lost our way
Caught up in a world of love, work and play
Listen can't you hear Him call you today
Would you be a coin in the hand of a King?
It would not be for you to choose
The object for which you would be used
But as the master saw fit each day
The price that is asked
You would be expected to pay

DOG OF BLUE

Would you be a coin in the hand of a King?
To be spent on a slave his freedom to bring
Stamped with His image,
Inscribed with His name
To be spent as a coin someone's freedom to gain

જીજીજીજીજીજીજીજીજીજીજીજીજીજી

2 Timothy 2:20
Now in a wealthy home there are not only gold and silver vessels, but also ones made of wood and of clay, and some are for honorable use, but others for ignoble use. 21 So if someone cleanses himself of such behavior, he will be a vessel for honorable use, set apart, useful for the Master, prepared for every good work. NET

Matthew 22:19-21
Show me the tribute money. And they brought unto him a penny. And he saith unto them, Whose is the image and subscription? They say unto him, Caesar's. Then saith he unto them, Render unto Caesar the things which are Caesar's and unto God the things that are God's.

જીજીજીજીજીજીજીજીજીજીજીજીજીજી

Everyday, God is looking for those who will volunteer. He desires willing volunteers who will quickly say yes. Someone today needs you. What could you do that would change someone's life today? There are people who need you. You could be that "coin." You could give someone freedom today. There are those in your life who may never experience what God can do, if you walk away. Be a coin. Be a smile. Be a hug. Will you be a coin in the hand of a king?

෨෨෨෨෨෨෨෨෨෨෨෨෨෨෨

Prayer
Lord use me as you see fit. I want to bring freedom to people's lives. I want to make a difference. So today I say yes. Today I offer myself to be spent by you as you see fit. Use me Lord.

෨෨෨෨෨෨෨෨෨෨෨෨෨෨෨

Notes

_____

_____

_____

_____

_____

_____

_____

෨෨෨෨෨෨෨෨෨෨෨෨෨෨෨

Prayer requests

_____
_____
_____
_____
_____
_____
_____
_____
_____

Day 9

VINEGAR DRINKERS

Pharisees are still alive;
You'll find them all around,
On old wine, they do thrive
For creeds and dogmas their renown
Always making up new rules,
But from the law, they claim,
"They're free"!
Seldom in response to faith, But fear!
Me-thinks,
They're eating from, "The wrong tree"!
They'll never drink that which is new,
For they're sure;
There is something in there, untrue.
But feast on stories, of revivals past
On anything new, suspicion cast
All that's worth knowing;
They have learned
But their old wine;
To vinegar has turned

DOG OF BLUE

ౠౠౠౠౠౠౠౠౠౠౠౠౠౠ

Jeremiah 48:11
"Moab has been at ease since his youth; He has also
been undisturbed, like wine on its dregs, And he has
not been emptied from vessel to vessel, Nor has he
gone into exile. Therefore he retains his flavor, And
his aroma has not changed. NKJV

James 3:14
But if ye have bitter envying and strife in your hearts,
glory not boast and lie not against the truth.

Job 12:1-2
Then Job answered and said, No doubt but ye are the
people, and wisdom will die with you.

Job 42:1-3
Then Job answered the Lord, and said, I know that
you canst do everything, and that no thought can be
withholden from thee. Who is he that hideth counsel
without knowledge?' therefore have I uttered that I
understood not; things too wonderful for me which I
knew not.

ౠౠౠౠౠౠౠౠౠౠౠౠౠౠ

If there is anything that turns people off, it is a Pharisee.
They act so high and mighty. Arrogance surrounds them
like a cloud. No one wants to be them or even to be near
them. Hypocrites flock together but even together they

fight as to who is the greatest, the best, or the most holy. One of their favorite pastimes is to criticize everyone around them. Everything around them is suspect, the way we worship, the way we sing, sometimes even the way we dress.

We must guard ourselves against this kind of attitude. Satan uses those thoughts to divide the church and split families. We should not forget that God is God. We are not! Therefore we haven't seen it all and we don't know it all. As Job acknowledged, some things are too wonderful for me to know.

ᏚᏚᏚᏚᏚᏚᏚᏚᏚᏚᏚᏚᏚᏚ

Prayer
Father, help me to live humbly. Lord I don't want to be a "know it all". I want to drink from your river of life that brings sweet peace. I don't want to be guilty of drinking vinegar. I don't want to be a sour person but one filled with your new wine, the life of your Spirit.

ᏚᏚᏚᏚᏚᏚᏚᏚᏚᏚᏚᏚᏚᏚ

Notes

_____
_____
_____
_____
_____
_____
_____
_____
_____

DOG OF BLUE

ഇഇഇഇഇഇഇഇഇഇഇഇഇഇ

Prayer Requests

_____

_____

_____

_____

_____

_____

_____

Day 10

BOUGH OVER THE WALL

Twas a seed that was planted, In a garden so fair
But off in a corner, Where no one seemed to care
Never received the praise, And accolades of all
But just seemed to be happy, Planted over by the wall
Year after year, it grew and grew
With some extra branches and blossoms, Yes more than a
few
But it kept on growing strong and tall
Till one day it reached, To the top of the wall
Then with some daring, And not really knowing how
On the other side of the wall, It let down a bough
And there, It spread it's branches so fair
With blossoms and fruit, for all to share
Then one morning, There was frost on the ground
And off in the distance, They heard a trumpet sound
What excitement there was, For all understood
The chief steward was coming, to take account of his goods
Bins filled with grain, And bushels with pears
The harvest was on, But some vines were bare
Crowns were given, To those with the most

To the cheers and applause, Of a heavenly host
But who should emerge, With the grand prize of all?
Why it was that forgotten about tree, In the corner so tall
Seems the gardener knew, What was hidden to all
About a bough that was spread, Down over the wall

ഓഓഓഓഓഓഓഓഓഓഓഓഓഓഓ

Genesis 49:22
Joseph is a fruitful bough, a fruitful bough near a
spring whose branches climb over the wall. NET

ഓഓഓഓഓഓഓഓഓഓഓഓഓഓഓ

Genesis tells us the story of when Jacob blessed his
children. To each one he prophesied. For Joseph he said
that he would be like branches growing over a wall. It
speaks of the triumph that Joseph made during difficult
times. It also speaks to us, that even when we face
adversity, we can be like Joseph and grow over the wall,
out of prison and out of our troubles. There is life on the
other side of the wall. There is life on the other side of our
problems. We can grow. We can better ourselves. We can
succeed. There is no wall too high, there is no problem too
difficult that you can not escape and continue to grow.

In Africa many of the houses have walls built around them.
Some have glass or metal spikes on top of the wall but
some have flowers that have grown up one side and down
another. At first you look and see the beauty of the flowers
and wonder why they would be chosen for security reasons.
It is not until you realize that those flowers have thorns that
would seriously wound a would-be climber. The flower

that grew over the wall was the strongest and most beautiful. It not only gave security but made the home even more lovely.

I want to be a bough over a wall. I want to grow up and over my troubles. I want the problems I have to make me strong and beautiful. You too can grow over the wall.

ෂාෂාෂාෂාෂාෂාෂාෂාෂාෂාෂාෂාෂාෂාෂා

Prayer
Lord, help me today. Sometimes my life seems overwhelming and yet I know you are with me. I want to be like Joseph. Life sometimes gets me down but I want to grow up and over. I want to be better than my problems. I want to be strong.

ෂාෂාෂාෂාෂාෂාෂාෂාෂාෂාෂාෂාෂාෂාෂා

Notes

_____
_____
_____
_____
_____
_____
_____
_____
_____

ෂාෂාෂාෂාෂාෂාෂාෂාෂාෂාෂාෂාෂාෂාෂා

Prayer Requests

_____
_____
_____
_____
_____
_____
_____
_____
_____
_____

Day 11

A PARADIGM SHIFT

A glimpse of His glory my burdens to lift
Can't wait to try out a new spiritual gift
But there's a whole new wine skin for you to fit in
His Paradigm shift is about to begin

Leave the old wine behind with the past generation
It will take more than revival to change our nation
More than a talented celebrity sensation
But a Paradigm shift for the New Creation

To old traditions and creeds How our hearts cling
Our security is certain under His wing
But from old creeds and ruts our hearts must pry
A great Paradigm shift is the Spirits cry

Yes there's a sea change coming* more than revival fire
More than a new song to play on our lyre
Out of our rut to a mesa higher,
A Paradigm shift is his desire

*a major transformation

ⴲⴲⴲⴲⴲⴲⴲⴲⴲⴲⴲⴲⴲⴲⴲ

Isaiah 43:18-20
Remember ye not the former things, neither consider the things of old. Behold, I will do a new thing; now it shall spring forth; shall ye not know it? I will even make a way in the wilderness, and rivers in the desert. The beast of the field shall honour me, the dragons and the owls: because I give waters in the wilderness, and rivers in the desert, to give drink to my people, my chosen

ⴲⴲⴲⴲⴲⴲⴲⴲⴲⴲⴲⴲⴲⴲⴲ

I have often heard that revival is what we need to change our country. While that sounds good and right, the problem is that our thoughts and focus have been on someone else changing and not on us. We need a whole new shift in how we pray. I need revival for me. You need revival for you. Not only do we need to recognize that it is we who need revival, we need to understand that God will not move like he did the last time. How revival looks today, will never be how it looked in the past. Expect the unexpected. Watch for God to move in ways you have never seen before.

ⴲⴲⴲⴲⴲⴲⴲⴲⴲⴲⴲⴲⴲⴲⴲ

Prayer
Lord, I need you to change me. Let your love and power fill me till I can take no more. I want you to permeate every part of me. Let the revival that you do in me flow out and touch others. Help me to get my eyes off from the failures of others and instead to focus on my need for change.

POEMS TO LIVE BY

ෂාෂාෂාෂාෂාෂාෂාෂාෂාෂාෂාෂාෂාෂාෂා

Notes

_____

_____

_____

_____

_____

_____

_____

_____

ෂාෂාෂාෂාෂාෂාෂාෂාෂාෂාෂාෂාෂාෂාෂා

Prayer Requests

_____

_____

_____

_____

_____

_____

_____

_____

Day 12

DECISION OR DISCOVERY

Scarcely did the vision fade
When a quality decision you had made
To follow the Lord, fulfill the call
Finish the course standing tall

But the assignment God has for you to do
Is not something for you to choose
If it were a matter of your volition
It would be easily polluted
By selfish ambition

Before the earth's foundation
It was planned
The portion of ground
On which you were to stand

And it's not for you to decide
The calling in which you are to abide
Equipping you with gifts and skill
Since before you were born
His purpose to fill

Like gold hidden beneath the earths crust
Awaiting your discovery
Committed to your trust
So start digging through the worldly debris
It's not your decision
But your discovery.

ഇ ഇ ഇ ഇ ഇ ഇ ഇ ഇ ഇ ഇ ഇ ഇ ഇ ഇ

Matthew 7:7
Ask and it will be given to you; seek and you will find;
knock and the door will be opened for you. For
everyone who asks receives, and the one who seeks
finds, and to the one who knocks, the door will be
opened. NET

ഇ ഇ ഇ ഇ ഇ ഇ ഇ ഇ ഇ ഇ ഇ ഇ ഇ ഇ

I love a scavenger hunt. I remember as a child, going to a
party and discovering that we were going to have a
scavenger hunt. We would run all over looking for one clue
after another. Sometimes we would look independently and
other times as a team. Running from place to place we
would pursue the grand prize of all, once it was a whole
pound of M&Ms! I guess the whole attraction was the end
prize but there was also a lot of fun in the chase. Of course
no matter who won, we all had a share.

 When I got older, my sister and I held a few scavenger
hunts ourselves. Only they weren't for children, we had
them as part of our woman's conferences. Even grown
women loved the hunt. There is a pleasure that comes

DOG OF BLUE

when you hunt for something wonderful and find it. God has surprises for each of us. Like a holy scavenger hunt he takes us on a journey through life. Every day becomes a page that is full of clues. One by one we make discoveries that leads to the next. Don't be discouraged if you feel you are stuck. Just don't give up! Seek and you will find.

෨෨෨෨෨෨෨෨෨෨෨෨෨෨෨~

Prayer
Father, I get so discouraged sometimes. It is hard to even believe that you have a special place for me in your kingdom. I want to have the faith to go on, to keep looking for my destiny but do I really have a destiny? I sometimes fear that I am just aimlessly wandering through life and that I have no purpose. I need some new clues today. Direct my day. Put me on the right path. I commit my life to you!

෨෨෨෨෨෨෨෨෨෨෨෨෨෨෨

Notes

_____
_____
_____
_____
_____
_____
_____

෨෨෨෨෨෨෨෨෨෨෨෨෨෨෨

Prayer Requests

_____

_____

_____

_____

_____

_____

_____

_____

Day 13

YOU ARE THE ANSWER

Long before you were carbon dated
For someone's dilemma you were created
Someone is now,   Struggling to survive
Awaiting for you,   With the answer to arrive

God gives Wealth
Not to spend on greed
But to help someone in dire need

God Gives Vision
Not to make you a spiritual celebrity
But to go to dark places and set the captives free

God Gives Wisdom
Not for you to win at chess
But help someone else to do their best

God Gives Faith
Not for your self to please
But to bring healing to someone's disease

POEMS TO LIVE BY

God Gives Joy
Let your laughter fill the air
But than go to others who are in despair

God Gives Love
Not to give you a good feeling
But to put your arm around someone
Whose heart needs healing

God Gives Acceptance
By now you should have expected
To receive others who have been rejected
In the gap between supply and demand
Find your place and faithfully stand

෴෴෴෴෴෴෴෴෴෴෴෴෴෴෴

Ezekiel 22:29-30
The people of the land have used oppression, and
exercised robbery, and have vexed the poor and
needy: yea, they have oppressed the stranger
wrongfully. 30 And I sought for a man among them,
that should make up the hedge, and stand in the gap
before me for the land, that I should not destroy it: but
I found none.

Ephesians 6:13-16
For this reason, take up the full armor of God so that
you may be able to stand your ground on the evil day,
and having done everything, to stand. Stand firm

therefore, by fastening the belt of truth around your waist, by putting on the breastplate of righteousness, by fitting your feet with the preparation that comes . from the good news of peace, and in all of this, by taking up the shield of faith with which you can extinguish all the flaming arrows of the evil one. NET

ഇ)ഇ)ഇ)ഇ)ഇ)ഇ)ഇ)ഇ)ഇ)ഇ)ഇ)ഇ)ഇ)ഇ)

God has gifts that he gives to each of us, like wisdom, peace in troubled times, and hope for tomorrow. But one of the most remarkable gifts of all is the ability to stand. In trouble, you can stand. In sickness you can stand. In pain you can stand. Having done everything, we can still exercise our faith and stand. The devil will try to knock you down but you can stand. He will try to take your peace but you can stand. He will try and take your joy but you can stand. Don't give up. Others depend on you to stand. Plant your feet firmly exercise your faith and stand.

ഇ)ഇ)ഇ)ഇ)ഇ)ഇ)ഇ)ഇ)ഇ)ഇ)ഇ)ഇ)ഇ)ഇ)

Prayer
Lord, help me to stand today. I don't know what I may face but I know that I can trust you. Whatever comes my way, my choice is to stand. I plant my feet firmly on your foundation and I know that you're with me. Thank you so much for your love and guidance. Today I will stand on you.

ഇ)ഇ)ഇ)ഇ)ഇ)ഇ)ഇ)ഇ)ഇ)ഇ)ഇ)ഇ)ഇ)ഇ)

Notes

_____
_____
_____
_____

_____

ಐಐಐಐಐಐಐಐಐಐಐಐಐಐ

Prayer Requests

_____
_____
_____
_____
_____

_____

Day 14

ROCK CRIED OUT

The cross could hold
What the grave could not
It was not the nails
But loves strong knot
In the tomb
Expected to remain
But none were there
To sing Hosannas refrain
So when the rock
Opened it's mouth to shout
Our lord just got up and
Walked out

൧൦൧൦൧൦൧൦൧൦൧൦൧൦൧൦

Luke 19:37b-40
The whole multitude of the disciples began to rejoice
and praise God with a loud voice for all the mighty
works that they had seen; Saying, Blessed be the
King that cometh in the name of the Lord: peace in

heaven and glory in the highest. And some of the Pharisees from among the multitude said unto him, Master rebuke thy disciples. And He answered and said unto them, I tell you that, if these should hold their peace, the stones would immediately cry out.

ଈଠଈଠଈଠଈଠଈଠଈଠଈଠଈଠଈଠଈଠଈଠଈଠ

Can you imagine rocks speaking? Just the thought makes me smile as I picture rocks with big eyes and shiny teeth, praising Jesus. Of course, in our limited mind, we know rocks have no voice and yet Jesus said that if we refuse to praise God, then nature would step up to the plate and worship. As unbelievable as this sounds it tells us of a much deeper place in the Spiritual realm. A place that we can not see with our eyes but is nevertheless real, where even rocks praise the Lord. Take just a moment and picture this, all nature crying out for the joy and glory of the Lord. How much more should we, being created in his image, cry out and praise him?

Spend some time today, thinking about the goodness of God. List the things he has done for you. Make an effort, when things don't go your way, to take your mind off of your problems and praise the Lord.

ଈଠଈଠଈଠଈଠଈଠଈଠଈଠଈଠଈଠଈଠଈଠଈଠ

Prayer
Lord I have to confess that there are times when I have forgotten to praise. Help me to be mindful of the price you paid for my salvation. Help me remember that you have given me life and that you are always with me. Keep my mind stayed on you and not on my problems. I choose to worship you. I choose to praise your great name.

DOG OF BLUE

జుజుజుజుజుజుజుజుజుజుజుజుజుజుజు

Notes

_____
_____
_____
_____
_____
_____
_____

జుజుజుజుజుజుజుజుజుజుజుజుజుజుజు

Prayer Requests

_____
_____
_____
_____
_____
_____
_____

Day 15

EVER LEARNING

Ever Learning and never coming to the truth
Some are hung over on doctrinal vermouth
Ever learning but in truth erosion
The victim of a preconceived notion
Ever Learning and never taking action
The church has reduced its power to a fraction
Ever learning but to come to the truth your un-able
You are in danger of believing a fable
Ever learning only to be lettered
You will leave behind those who were fettered
Ever learning it's a family tradition
Tis seldom worth what you pay in tuition
Ever learning just to tease your brain
With so little to work with you could go insane
Ever learning with pride you will swell
Like a number five turtle in a number three shell
Ever learning trying to make points with God
You may as well carve a totem from a log
Ever learning just to be cool
You will no doubt become an educated fool

DOG OF BLUE

Ever learning so more money you can earn
Your wages will never equal your yearn
Ever learning;
Ah, the mysteries of the treasured pearl to unlock
But of those who find, most faint with sticker shock
Few ever sell all to make it their possession
Instead they just sign up for more education

ഇന്ദ്രന്ദ്രന്ദ്രന്ദ്രന്ദ്രന്ദ്രന്ദ്രന്ദ്രന്ദ്രന്ദ്ര

2 Timothy 3:7
Such women are always seeking instruction, yet
never able to arrive at a knowledge of the truth. NET

ഇന്ദ്രന്ദ്രന്ദ്രന്ദ്രന്ദ്രന്ദ്രന്ദ്രന്ദ്രന്ദ്രന്ദ്ര

Today, make a choice to take all the knowledge you have of
God and put it into practice. Be filled with the Holy Spirit.
Praise the Lord for who he is and not just for what he does.
Love your enemies. Set aside your own agenda. Be a
living sacrifice.

While education is great, we must always endeavor to keep
the "main thing" the "main thing". Have you ever heard
people say that their marriage didn't work out, because they
weren't "in love" with their mate! They will tell you they
never were in love with him or her, but only " in love" with
being "in love". Well it is like that with knowledge. Some
people are so caught up in the learning process that they
forget the truth of the knowledge they are seeking. They
love the process, the schooling, the research and yet they
forget that there is a goal - the truth they are seeking.

Gaining knowledge becomes more exciting than the truth of that knowledge itself.

It's so easy these days to watch a great preacher on TV, read a good book, or go to a great seminar. Opportunities to learn more about God or the Bible are plentiful and yet our culture is falling further and further away from the Lord. It is sad that our opportunities to learn more about God, have not brought us to a place of spiritual revolution. Our country should be gaining spiritual ground everyday and yet it is only too obvious that we are falling further and further away from the truth we are studying. Why is that? It is because we never come to the knowledge of the truth. We never arrive to the place of becoming a living sacrifice, holy and acceptable to our Lord.

ะด ะด ะด ะด ะด ะด ะด ะด ะด ะด ะด ะด ะด ะด ะด

Prayer
Lord, I have learned so much about you and yet sometimes my life doesn't reflect what I know. I have fallen short. Help me oh Lord, to keep my eyes on you. Help me to keep my eyes on the goal and not only on the journey. I want to be captivated by you and not just on my journey.

ะด ะด ะด ะด ะด ะด ะด ะด ะด ะด ะด ะด ะด ะด ะด

Notes

_____
_____
_____
_____
_____
_____
_____

ഇന്ദ്രന്ദ്രന്ദ്രന്ദ്രന്ദ്രന്ദ്രന്ദ്രന്ദ്ര

Prayer Requests

_____
_____
_____
_____
_____

Day 16

PUT YOUR CANOE IN THE WATER

My hour in the sun
What steps must I take
The call to fulfill
His will – to facilitate

In prayer and praise
Your skills and gifts hone
Wait on the Lord
And answer the phone

A living sacrifice
Let your will crumble
Sit with the lowly
He gives grace to the humble

For some great ship to come in
Don't fritter and faultier
Be faithful in little
And put your canoe in the water

ꜱꜱꜱꜱꜱꜱꜱꜱꜱꜱꜱꜱꜱꜱ

Luke 16:10
The one who is faithful in a very little is also faithful in much, and the one who is dishonest in a very little is also dishonest in much. NET

Romans 12:1-2
Therefore I exhort you, brothers and sisters, by the mercies of God, to present your bodies as a sacrifice - alive, holy, and pleasing to God - which is your reasonable service. Do not be conformed to this present world, but be transformed by the renewing of your mind, so that you may test and approve what is the will of God - what is good and well-pleasing and perfect. NET

ꜱꜱꜱꜱꜱꜱꜱꜱꜱꜱꜱꜱꜱꜱ

I am often asked, "What is God's will for my life. How do I know what to do?" I think every person who loves God has asked that same question at one time or another in their life. How do we know the will of God for our life?

Stories of successful people seem to go back to two things that they did to be successful. They worked harder and with more passion that those around them. Secondly they happened to be in the right place at the right time. I love this little poem because it expresses those same things. Being a living sacrifice is the same thing as giving everything you've got to achieve your goal. Putting your canoe into the water, illustrates making the step to push off into the water that will direct your path. In other words, taking you to the right place at the right time. This is how I live. We have to find the place where passion and trust meet. This is how we find God's will. We live wholly unto him, having no regrets. And trusting as we push out to sea knowing that wherever the current of God flows, will be his will for my life.

ಐಐಐಐಐಐಐಐಐಐಐಐಐಐಐ

Prayer
Lord help me to prepare for tomorrow and trust you at the same time. Keep my mind from stress and the fear of the unknown. I know you have a plan for me and so I will walk with you day by day until I find that plan.

ಐಐಐಐಐಐಐಐಐಐಐಐಐಐಐ

Notes

_____
_____
_____
_____
_____
_____
_____
_____
_____
_____

ಐಐಐಐಐಐಐಐಐಐಐಐಐಐಐ

Prayer Requests

_____

_____

_____

_____

_____

_____

_____

_____

_____

_____

_____

Day 17

PIONEERS NEEDED

There are realms in the Spirit
That man has not discovered
To these a blanket
The enemy or' our minds has covered

"The canon is complete;
I've read it through and through
All there is to know about God I can tell you"

But Dan and Paul saw things they could not tell
There's coming a time that we will know them well
Like explores of old saying the world was round
There are realms of the Spirit yet to be found
The surface in prayer and faith we've only just scratched
There's eggs of revelation that have not yet been hatched
But for new worlds to find and ideas to be born
As explores of old you'll be laughed to scorn
And some may even be crucified
For saying there's lands beyond the tide
Leaving family and homes great risk they did take

DOG OF BLUE

But like pioneers we need to leave the land of
Scofield* and Dake *
No more Spiritual Realms to discover
we have it all down pat
Is the equivalent of saying the world is flat

*Two well known study Bibles with opinionated study notes.

ഌ ഌ ഌ ഌ ഌ ഌ ഌ ഌ ഌ ഌ ഌ ഌ ഌ ഌ ഌ

John 16:12-16
I have many more things to say to you, but you
cannot bear them now. But when he, the Spirit of
truth, comes, he will guide you into all truth. For he
will not speak on his own authority, but will speak
whatever he hears, and will tell you what is to come.
He will glorify me, because he will receive from me
what is mine and will tell it to you. Everything that the
Father has is mine; that is why I said the Spirit will
receive from me what is mine and will tell it to you. 16
In a little while you will see me no longer; again after a
little while, you will see me. NET

2 Timothy 1:6
Because of this I remind you to rekindle God's gift that
you possess through the laying on of my hands. NET

ഌ ഌ ഌ ഌ ഌ ഌ ഌ ഌ ഌ ഌ ഌ ഌ ഌ ഌ ഌ

In studying American history, I see passion in the lives of the men and women who explore new places of wildernesses. They suffered sickness, hunger and sometimes even death. They pressed on until there was no more strength in them. They changed the world. They discovered new places. They found their own promised land. I wonder what the world would be like if we pursued God in this same way. Would we change the world? Would we discover new revivals? Would we see the kingdom of God coming in all of it's glory? I believe we would. I want to discover new things from God. I want to have fresh revelation from his word. Just like the explorers of old, I want to have an impact on the generations who follow me.

Today press into the Word of God. Stir up your passion. Use every opportunity to pray and stir up God's gift inside of you.

~ଈଈଈଈଈଈଈଈଈଈଈଈଈଈଈ

Prayer
Lord, I don't want to be a mediocre Christian. I don't want to just listen to what others say about you, I want to experience you for myself. Help me to hear your voice and dig deeper in your word. I want to make an impact on my world.

ଈଈଈଈଈଈଈଈଈଈଈଈଈଈ

Notes

_____
_____
_____
_____
_____
_____
_____

ഔ ഔ ഔ ഔ ഔ ഔ ഔ ഔ ഔ ഔ ഔ ഔ ഔ ഔ ഔ

Prayer Requests

_____
_____
_____
_____
_____
_____

Day 18

FRESH WATER

Building cisterns that can hold no water
Laying bricks with greedy mortar
Making it look pleasant to the eye
But even in a rain you will find it dry
For two evils man stands before God guilty
Forsaking the fresh and saving the filthy
The law of the Spirit of life can be found
From the Tree of Life that grew in Eden's ground
To Revelations river flowing from the throne
And with the water what we have done
Will make us bold or retreat
The day we stand before the judgment seat
Have we drank of the Fountain
Making us new creations
Turning into a river flowing out to all nations
Or Like Adam behind some leaves do we cower
Trading a spring for an afternoon shower
And building a dike to control it's power
No don't be content
With water that's stale
Like the woman at the well
Behind leave your pail

Jeremiah 2:13
"For My people have committed two evils: They have
forsaken Me, The fountain of living waters, To hew for
themselves cisterns, Broken cisterns That can hold no
water.

Revelation 22:1-5
Then the angel showed me the river of the water of
life - water as clear as crystal - pouring out from the
throne of God and of the Lamb, flowing down the
middle of the city's main street. On each side of the
river is the tree of life producing twelve kinds of fruit,
yielding its fruit every month of the year. Its leaves are
for the healing of the nations. And there will no longer
be any curse, and the throne of God and the Lamb
will be in the city. His servants will worship him, 4 and
they will see his face, and his name will be on their
foreheads. Night will be no more, and they will not
need the light of a lamp or the light of the sun,
because the Lord God will shine on them, and they
will reign forever and ever. NET

John 7:37-38
On the last day of the feast, the greatest day, Jesus
stood up and shouted out, "If anyone is thirsty, let him
come to me, and 38 let the one who believes in me
drink. Just as the scripture says, 'From within him will
flow rivers of living water.'" NET

ᘓᘓᘓᘓᘓᘓᘓᘓᘓᘓᘓᘓᘓᘓᘓ

An old song says, "There's a river of life flowing out from
me. It makes the lame to walk and the blind to see....." It
goes on to tell of the power of that river and then it tells the
water to spring up within our souls. This wonderful
amazing river of life flows out from those who have given
their life to the Lord Jesus. This river brings health and
healing, peace and joy, life and that more abundantly. Take
a few minutes to think about this river. Close your eyes and
speak to that river. Say, "River of God, flow through me.
Bring me peace and direction for my day. May I be an
instrument of life as this river of God flows through me."

ᘓᘓᘓᘓᘓᘓᘓᘓᘓᘓᘓᘓᘓᘓᘓ

Prayer
Lord, I need your river to flow through me. If I have done
anything to stop the flow, tell me. I want a continued flow
that gives me peace. This world is full of troubles and
things to be afraid of but you oh Lord have given me peace.
You Lord Jesus, have promised me living water.

ᘓᘓᘓᘓᘓᘓᘓᘓᘓᘓᘓᘓᘓᘓᘓ

Notes

_____

_____

_____

_____

_____

_____

_____

_____

_____

DOG OF BLUE

ଯଡଯଡଯଡଯଡଯଡଯଡଯଡଯଡଯଡଯଡଯଡଯଡ

Prayer Requests

_____

_____

_____

_____

_____

_____

_____

_____

Day 19

PEARLS

The trials of life
Often unbearable irritations
But the pearls that result
Are priceless creations
Pearls from oysters
In the market are sold
But Pearls of the Spirit
Can not be purchased with Gold
When you see one forming
That looks especially nice
Sell all to acquire
It's well worth the price
Tho the trials of life
Are the scorn of the world
The entrance to heaven
Is a gate of pearl
And pearls are beautiful
And a delight to be worn
But few will give
Them time to form

DOG OF BLUE

But like pearls from oysters
The Word would warn you
Only wear them among those
Who understand their value
The treasures of darkness
Will glitter in the light
But those still in darkness
Are a repulsed by the sight
The sight of pearls
To some is near magic
Transforms them into hogs
The party turns tragic
So before you wear your pearls
Better check your guest list
Watch for those who'll
Get reckless with your necklace

જી જી જી જી જી જી જી જી જી જી જી જી જી જી જી

Matthew 13:45-46
Again the Kingdom of heaven is like a merchant man,
seeking fine pearls. Who, when he had found one
pearl of great price, went and sold all that he had, and
bought it.

Matthew 7:6
Give not that which is holy unto dogs, neither cast
your pearls before swine, lest they trample them
under their feet, and turn again and rend you.

POEMS TO LIVE BY

Isaiah 45:3a
I will give thee the treasures of darkness, and hidden riches of secret places,

ဆဆဆဆဆဆဆဆဆဆဆဆဆဆဆ

My dad and I have had many occasions to visit Green Hills, a shopping area in Manila Philippines. Millions of pearls hang from tightly situated boutiques. One could spend hours just going from one pearl vendor to another. However there are only a few shops where the most costly pearls are for sale. These pearls are fashioned on delicate pieces of velvet and fastened with gold clasps. Every time I visit, I am reminded of Jesus' words when he spoke about the Kingdom of Heaven being like a merchant looking for the pearl of great price. I imagine looking for the greatest pearl, the one that shines the best, that has the most beautiful luster. If I ever bought such a pearl, I would keep it in a special box or display it behind glass. I would never let a child play with it, least of all wear it while working in a barnyard with pigs.

When I think of these pearls, I think about the pearls that God has made from my life. Difficulties and problems in my life produce my "treasures in darkness." These are the nuggets of gold or pearls that I find from troubles in my life. They serve to remind me that no matter my situation, God has a gift for me. The darkness of life produces the purest of gems. We should always look for them. Too many people look at the trouble and never find the pearl. Look for the pearl. Don't be satisfied till you find it. Never come out of a difficulty empty handed.

ဆဆဆဆဆဆဆဆဆဆဆဆဆဆဆ

DOG OF BLUE

Prayer
Lord, keep my mind stayed on you...help me to fix my eyes
on what you have for me today. I may face difficulties but I
know that no matter what my situation, you have never left
me alone and you have a treasure laid out just for me. Help
me to never give up. To push on pursuing you no matter
what comes my way.

ഇരഇരഇരഇരഇരഇരഇരഇരഇരഇരഇരഇര

Notes

_____
_____
_____
_____
_____
_____
_____

ഇരഇരഇരഇരഇരഇരഇരഇരഇരഇരഇരഇര

Prayer Requests

_____
_____
_____
_____
_____
_____
_____

Day 20

THE KINGDOM

The Gospel of the Kingdom
Will Save and Create
Two classes of People
Those who Love and Those who Hate

This message our Lord did relate
If they persecute me don't think you will escape
They will love to death
Or your Life they will take

And Between Mercy and Unforgivingness
Let us not vacillate
Love your enemies
And Never let the Sabers Shake

The devils task
Keeping you trapped in the past
In anger and bitterness
From God's blessing you'll stand fast

DOG OF BLUE

Locked by the devil
behind hells gate
Or the Strong Hold of God
The choice you must make

By Forgetting and Forgiving
The Kingdom you can take
Yes the message of the Kingdom
In you will create
the Knowledge of
What to Love, and what to Hate

೮೦೮೦೮೦೮೦೮೦೮೦೮೦೮೦೮೦೮೦೮೦೮೦೮೦೮೦

Matthew 6:14-15
For if you forgive others their sins, your heavenly
Father will also forgive you. But if you do not forgive
others, your Father will not forgive you your sins. NET

೮೦೮೦೮೦೮೦೮೦೮೦೮೦೮೦೮೦೮೦೮೦೮೦೮೦೮೦

It used to be said that to forgive is to forget. Sometimes
that is easier said than done. I have discovered that
sometimes we have to be willing to forget but the forgetting
takes time and often requires repeated forgiveness. Some
people don't want to forget because they fear the offense
will happen again. For this reason they repeat in their mind
the offense. Mistakenly they think that by remembering,
they are keeping the wrong done to them alive. Instead
they are keeping the pain and anxiety alive in their heart as
they rehearse every wound. Believe me, the only one who
suffers is you.

Have you ever gone shopping and after a day in the mall, come home singing songs you haven't sung in years or humming a tune you didn't even like? Have you ever wondered how to get those melodies out of your head? Sing another song. It is that simple. Sing a different song. It is the same with forgiving and forgetting. Every time you are reminded of something you are finding hard to forgive, fill your mind with different ideas. Sing a song. Read the Word of God. Work at forgiving and forgetting. It will change your life!

⁕⁕⁕⁕⁕⁕⁕⁕⁕⁕⁕⁕⁕⁕⁕

Prayer
Lord, so often I try to forget but I feel so broken inside. I try to forgive but I can't get the memories of hurt to go away. Please help me today, as I make an effort to forget. I choose to forgive and forget. Fill my mind with your goodness. Make your word come alive in me. I trust in you!

⁕⁕⁕⁕⁕⁕⁕⁕⁕⁕⁕⁕⁕⁕⁕

Notes

_____

_____

_____

_____

_____

_____

⁕⁕⁕⁕⁕⁕⁕⁕⁕⁕⁕⁕⁕⁕⁕

DOG OF BLUE

Prayer Requests

_____

_____

_____

_____

_____

_____

Day 21

GIVE THEM TO JESUS

You will encounter difficulties
Everyone has their share
But let not their anxiety
Drive you to despair
On the Lord cast your burden
His yoke is light indeed
When we carry his
From ours we are freed
Let not difficulties worry you to the bone
But let them be an occasion
to let His glory be shown.

∽∽∽∽∽∽∽∽∽∽∽∽∽∽∽

Mat. 11:28-30
Come unto me all you who are weary and burdened
and I will give you rest. Take my yoke on you and
learn from me, because I am gentle and humble in
heart, and you will find rest for your souls. For my
yoke is easy to bear and my load is not hard to
carry.""

DOG OF BLUE

⊱⊰⊱⊰⊱⊰⊱⊰⊱⊰⊱⊰⊱⊰⊱⊰⊱⊰

Worry has never done anyone any good. It only causes added anxiety and fear. Jesus said we could come to him and he would carry our burdens. We trade our emotional pain for his peace and his rest. It's not being irresponsible, to resist worry and rest in Jesus. It's freedom. It's life. And it's the best thing we can do. We are unable to add even one moment to our life by worrying but instead we cut our life short and lose our effectiveness.

The next time you are tempted to worry, spend a few minutes with the Lord. Tell him your troubles. Leave your cares with him. He will not only take your burdens but he actually wants them.

⊱⊰⊱⊰⊱⊰⊱⊰⊱⊰⊱⊰⊱⊰⊱⊰⊱⊰

Prayer
Lord, today my life is filled with troubles and problems. I know there is nothing I can do to make things turn out all right. Fear sometimes grabs my spirit and I feel lost in my troubles. Please take my fear and worry. Replace my stress with your peace. I love and trust you today. No matter what comes my way, I trust you to take care of it all.

⊱⊰⊱⊰⊱⊰⊱⊰⊱⊰⊱⊰⊱⊰⊱⊰⊱⊰

Notes

_____

_____

_____

_____

_____

_____

_____

ഔഔഔഔഔഔഔഔഔഔഔഔഔ

Prayer Requests

_____

_____

_____

_____

_____

_____

_____

Day 22

JUDAS

Judas with the wrong crowd did hang
Betrayal will always equate with his name

Distraught over the deed he had done
He confessed his sin but to the wrong one

The blood of Jesus for him was shed
Not seeing it's value he took his own life instead

This same scenario has often been played
When a mess of their lives people have made

Of Christ's blood They have their doubt
Their religion tells them See to it yourself
And so with Judas…They… hang out

₰₰₰₰₰₰₰₰₰₰₰₰₰₰

Matthew 27:5
"he (Judas) cast down the pieces of silver in the temple and departed, and went and hanged himself"

ഔ ഔ ഔ ഔ ഔ ഔ ഔ ഔ ഔ ഔ ഔ ഔ ഔ ഔ ഔ

How sad it is to read the account of Judas. He had it all. He learned from the Master himself and yet when he failed, he felt there was no hope. He walked away from the Lord and fell in a pit of despair. However that is only half of the story. Peter also betrayed the Lord, that same night. Yet instead of running away in shame, he ran to Jesus.

If you find you have failed, don't run away and hide. Jesus has provided forgiveness and restitution. No matter what you have done, don't follow after Judas. There is hope. There is a new day for you. Nothing is too bad or too wicked that you can't be redeemed and restored. Follow the example of Peter. Run to Jesus. He can make everything right.

ഔ ഔ ഔ ഔ ഔ ഔ ഔ ഔ ഔ ഔ ഔ ഔ ഔ ഔ ഔ

Prayer
Lord, I know I have failed. Like Judas, I want to run from you. Change me Lord. Take away the bad and create in me a new life. Lord I don't want to run from you but sometimes I feel so ashamed. Today I choose to run to you. Change me.

ഔ ഔ ഔ ഔ ഔ ഔ ഔ ഔ ഔ ഔ ഔ ഔ ഔ ഔ ഔ

Notes

_____

_____

_____

_____

_____

ഌഌഌഌഌഌഌഌഌഌഌഌഌഌ

Prayer Requests

_____

_____

_____

_____

_____

Day 23

HIDDEN AGENDA

When poverty and bareness
Put our faith to the test
And over your sad condition
The devil would jest.
From you and your friends
It will bring out the best
But when banners are flying
And you enjoy great success
The monsters of Lock Ness
Will be brought to the crest
Agendas that in bareness
Were concealed
In time of success
Will be revealed
With a morsel before
So glad to get by
Now they demand
A bigger slice of the pie
Victorious warriors
In the battles of Need
Often fall to the demon of Greed

DOG OF BLUE

Philippines 4:10-13
I have great joy in the Lord because now at last you have again expressed your concern for me. (Now I know you were concerned before but had no opportunity to do anything.) I am not saying this because I am in need, for I have learned to be content in any circumstance. I have experienced times of need and times of abundance. In any and every circumstance I have learned the secret of contentment, whether I go satisfied or hungry, have plenty or nothing. I am able to do all things through the one who strengthens me. Nevertheless, you did well to share with me in my trouble. NET

ﮙﮙﮙﮙﮙﮙﮙﮙﮙﮙﮙﮙﮙﮙﮙ

My dad once told me that the testing of success is greater than the test for failure. So often people forget the Lord when they are prospering. I have seen many people who are faithful to God, faithful in fellowship with other believers, and faithful in tithes and offerings during times of need. They would come to church faithfully, asking for prayer. They needed a job, a place to live, or they had health problems. Then as soon as they felt better, got the job or new house, they no longer "needed" the Lord and they stopped coming around. They got caught in the trap of success.

I have a friend who just recently went through this very thing. We had warned him repeatedly that as soon as he got a job, that he shouldn't forget us and most importantly not to forget the Lord Jesus. Unfortunately he fell into the trap of success. Dear friend. Take this warning to heart. Don't let this become you!

જીજીજીજીજીજીજીજીજીજીજીજીજીજી

Prayer
Dear Lord, I have many needs in my life. I know that it is easy to forget you. The successes of life have caught me in the past and I fear they will again. Don't allow finances, or a job steal your place in my life. I need you more than ever. Help me Lord to keep my priorities in the right place.

જીજીજીજીજીજીજીજીજીજીજીજીજીજી

Notes

_____
_____
_____
_____
_____
_____
_____
_____

જીજીજીજીજીજીજીજીજીજીજીજીજીજી

DOG OF BLUE

Prayer Requests

_____

_____

_____

_____

_____

_____

_____

_____

Day 24

ALL YOU NEED

No one wants to be broke
We all want to have a plenty
Of gadgets and gizmos - the things of this world
And a bank that is bulging with money
Fame and fortune, friends without end
To be stripped of these none of want
But you'll never know that
Jesus is all you need
Until He is all you have got

ഇ ഇ ഇ ഇ ഇ ഇ ഇ ഇ ഇ ഇ ഇ ഇ ഇ ഇ ഇ

Psalms 39:7
"And now, Lord, what wait I for? My hope is in Thee.

Psalms 27:10
When my father and mother forsake me then the Lord
will take me up

ഇ ഇ ഇ ഇ ഇ ഇ ഇ ഇ ഇ ഇ ഇ ഇ ഇ ഇ ഇ

DOG OF BLUE

Years ago, when I lived in West Africa, I had a friend who lived in a cardboard box. He was washing cars for a living and making almost no money. Yet he was a very happy man. He told me he loved Jesus and it was obvious that Jesus and his cardboard box were all he had. By USA standards he was broke. He didn't have all the things that I have in my home yet he was happy. Jesus was all he had and he was happy.

Today my home is in New York and the lifestyles of people around me are vastly different from my friend in the box. Television ads bombard those who watch with new gadgets everyday. One minute spent watching causes one to desire the latest wonder, pondering how we were able to live life without it. A credit card is whipped out of the wallet and our latest toy is promised to arrive in just a few days. With excitement the box is ripped open and much to our dismay, the joy doesn't last. Maybe the next "latest greatest" will do the trick and fill the emptiness within. But it never will, because all we need is Jesus. Nothing can take his place.

ଽଠଽଠଽଠଽଠଽଠଽଠଽଠଽଠଽଠଽଠଽଠଽଠଽଠ

Prayer
Lord, help me to keep my eyes on you. It is so easy to get sucked in and covet what I see on TV or in my neighbors home. Help me to be satisfied with you and only you. I don't want to fill my life with empty things but with what truly matters. It is too easy to forget you when my life is full of clutter and clutter does not satisfy. I know that all I need is you!

ଽଠଽଠଽଠଽଠଽଠଽଠଽଠଽଠଽଠଽଠଽଠଽଠଽଠ

Notes

_____

_____

_____

_____

_____

_____

_____

_____

෨෨෨෨෨෨෨෨෨෨෨෨෨෨෨

Prayer Requests

_____

_____

_____

_____

_____

_____

_____

_____

Day 25

THE CHIEF IS IN THE CAMP

Once in a dream at dawn I came
to the banks of the Genesee above the Caneada plain.
And there a village of Indians I saw
in their lodges of Elm, braves, children and squaw.
And as I viewed this scene of old
a message for us was about to unfold.
For there in the camp was a chaotic scene
a mass of activity without any scheme.
Some were coming some were going
some were reaping while others were sowing.
Some were crying while others were glad
and many were fighting over the things they had.
Tempers were flaring and insults exchanged,
over senseless things as status and fame.
And many were hoarding all they could store,
for fear of a famine or in case of a war.
My heart filled with sorrow, as I began to cry
all hope for these people seemed long past gone by.
Was there none to help? But oh!

On the opposite bank of the Genesee
stood a warrior chief like a mighty oak tree.
His eyes were aflame, his right hand held a bow,
dripping with blood fresh from the foe.
A thousand warriors stood at his side
and he leaped the gorge with only a stride.
Than there was silence for a moment no more,
and their cries and insults turned to a roar.
The Chief Is In The Camp
With a shout of His voice and raising his hand
they came to their feet and stood as one man.
Shoulder to shoulder in one accord,
they looked upon him as though he were lord.
They stopped their sowing they stopped their reaping
they ceased their fighting they stopped their weeping.
And without turning around to things left behind,
he led them away a new camp to find.
And than I awoke and thought of my Lord,
and His body the church both here and abroad.
And all I could think and all I could pray, was
Lord come into our camp today.

ഇൗഇൗഇൗഇൗഇൗഇൗഇൗഇൗഇൗഇൗഇൗഇൗഇൗഇൗഇൗ

Numbers 23:21
He has not looked on iniquity in Jacob, nor has he
seen trouble in Israel. The Lord their God is with
them; his acclamation as king is among them. NET

DOG OF BLUE

Zephaniah 3:17
"The LORD thy God in the midst of thee is mighty. He
will save, he will rejoice over thee with joy; he will rest
in his love, he will joy over thee with singing."

Deuteronomy 23:14
For the Lord your God walks about in the middle of
your camp to deliver you and defeat your enemies for
you. Therefore your camp should be holy, so that he
does not see anything indecent among you and turn
away from you. NET

ഇഇഇഇഇഇഇഇഇഇഇഇഇഇഇ

The illustration in this poem is so vivid. I can see the
church doing exactly as the village in the dream. I've had
the privilege of visiting many churches and I have noticed
that whether large or small, every church is the same.
There will be people who come, weary from their week.
Some will come sick in their body or mind, seeking a
healing or at least some rest from their torment. I see
families bickering and even old friends finding fault with
each other. But when the music starts and the songs begin
to swell. I see hands lifted up to King Jesus as he takes his
place as Lord. Something happens when we acknowledge
that Jesus is King and we begin to worship him. We set
aside (or we should) all of the things that distract us. We
leave behind our burdens and cares. We let go of our
problems and worship the King who has entered our camp.

ഇഇഇഇഇഇഇഇഇഇഇഇഇഇഇ

POEMS TO LIVE BY

Prayer
Lord help me to truly worship you. Help me to become so
caught up in you that grumbling and complaining ceases.
Helps me to focus my energy on you and not on other
people or my problems. You are the King. Come into my
camp today!

ഈഈഈഈഈഈഈഈഈഈഈഈഈഈഈ

Notes

_____

_____

_____

_____

_____

_____

_____

ഈഈഈഈഈഈഈഈഈഈഈഈഈഈഈ

Prayer Requests

_____

_____

_____

_____

_____

_____

_____

Day 26

DANCING FAITH

Hope hears the music of the future
Faith breaks into a dance
To that heavenly rhythm his step is sure
But the world thinks it's a hyped up trance
Of those heavenly strains they hear not a sound
While the man of faith is 'getting down'

When that melody is heard from a far off land
Some would venture to clap their hand
To step out in faith many are slow
Tis well enough for them to tap their toe
But if you would move mountains
All fears and doubt shrug
Get out on the floor and cut a rug

When the music starts Faith has a reaction
Not content to sit he must take action
That music of the future Hope will hear
Faith will dance with a step that's sure
Those heavenly strains others hear not a sound
But the man of faith is dancing around

Yes Faith dances to what Hope has an ear
Of peers and failure he has no fear
His destiny is not given to chance
When Hope hears that music
His feet start to dance

ഉ൹ഉ൹ഉ൹ഉ൹ഉ൹ഉ൹ഉ൹ഉ൹

2 Samuel 6:14
Now David, wearing a linen ephod, was dancing with all his strength before the Lord. NET

Psalms 30:10-12
Hear, O Lord, and have mercy on me! O Lord, deliver me!" Then you turned my lament into dancing; you removed my sackcloth and covered me with joy. So now my heart will sing to you and not be silent; O Lord my God, I will always give thanks to you. NET

ഉ൹ഉ൹ഉ൹ഉ൹ഉ൹ഉ൹ഉ൹ഉ൹

There is something about dancing that sets a spirit free. The cares of the world are forgotten when toes begin to tap and hands begin to clap to the music, when our minds begin to flow with a melody and the words go deep inside of our being. God created music to bring us peace, joy, hope, passion and so much more. Today, turn on some music, sing a song of praise to the Lord. Clap your hands and move your feet....find joy in the beat and loose yourself in the words. Become like King David. Dance with all of your strength.

ಕುಡುಕುಡುಕುಡುಕುಡುಕುಡುಕುಡುಕುಡುಕುಡುಕುಡುಕುಡು

Prayer

Father, stir up my faith. I want to join in with the angels who rejoice around your throne. I want to be stirred to action. Don't allow me to be ruled by my fears but encourage me in faith. I know my destiny is in your hands. What a joy it is, to know that I can trust you.

ಕುಡುಕುಡುಕುಡುಕುಡುಕುಡುಕುಡುಕುಡುಕುಡುಕುಡುಕುಡು

Notes

_____

_____

_____

_____

_____

_____

_____

ಕುಡುಕುಡುಕುಡುಕುಡುಕುಡುಕುಡುಕುಡುಕುಡುಕುಡುಕುಡು

Prayer Requests

_____

_____

_____

_____

Day 27

WORDS SESQUIPEDALIAN

Some words we use are sesquipedalian
The meaning of which to many are alien
It's all because of the Tower of Babble
Where God confused the language
And man invented Scrabble
If there is any value in this poetry
You say you can't summarize
Well did the rest of your day
Win a Nobel Prize?
If you've read this far
There is one thing plain
Some people are not hard to entertain
The gospel of Christ
Can be understood by a child
But phraseology and theology
Have our understanding beguiled
Ambiguous terms the truth to hide
The devil uses
So folks won't know that he's lied
For some they

DOG OF BLUE

Make them appear dignified
Makes their pride shine
For to the ears of some, poetry is please'n
But I fear this is more rhyme than reason
A feeble fable my padre would patter
And if sesquipedalian you don't know the meaning
It doesn't matter!

ॐॐॐॐॐॐॐॐॐॐॐॐॐॐॐ

Matthew 19:13-15
Then little children were brought to him for him to lay his hands on them and pray. But the disciples scolded those who brought them. But Jesus said, "Let the little children come to me and do not try to stop them, for the kingdom of heaven belongs to such as these." And he placed his hands on them and went on his way. NET

Jeremiah 29:11
For I know what I have planned for you, 'says the Lord. I have plans to prosper you not to harm you. I have plans to give you a future filled with hope. NET

ॐॐॐॐॐॐॐॐॐॐॐॐॐॐॐ

Sometimes we forget the simplicity of the Gospel. In fact the Gospel is so simple that even little children can understand it. Jesus came to earth as a man and died for the sins of the world. Three days after he died, he came back to life, having broken the chains of death on our lives. He sits at the right of the Father interceding for you and I. His Holy Spirit he sent to fill us with his presence while we wait here on earth for the day he will say, "Well done good and faithful servant."

God has a plan for our lives. We don't have to know all the different theologies or take part in great debates to understand this. These things just doesn't matter. What does matter can be summed up in one little Sunday School song, "Jesus loves me this I know."

છાજીજાજીજાજીજાજીજાજીજાજીજાજીજા

Prayer
Lord help me to rest in your simplicity. You love me, and you have a plan for my life. You are with me even when I don't feel like you are.

છાજીજાજીજાજીજાજીજાજીજાજીજાજીજા

Notes

_____
_____
_____
_____
_____
_____
_____

છાજીજાજીજાજીજાજીજાજીજાજીજાજીજા

Prayer Requests

_____

_____

_____

_____

_____

_____

_____

Day 28

PRISONERS OF HOPE

With shackles bound to hand and feet
They sink into the mire deeper
Without a drop to refresh their soul,
They sink deeper still into a water-less hole
Bound with chains of sin and despair
Without a hope they've not a prayer

And then to the bottom of the pit it came,
Like the morning dew or a fresh spring rain
The blood of the covenant
From the lamb that was slain
He brought them out to the morning air
A double portion would be their share

And alas they find they're prisoners again
Shackled to the one that died for them
But no longer does despair over them gloat
Today they have become
Prisoners of Hope

಼಼಼಼಼಼಼಼಼಼಼಼಼಼಼

Zechariah 9:11-12
As for thee also, by the blood of thy covenant I have sent forth thy prisoners out of the pit wherein is no water. Turn you to the strong hold, ye prisoners of hope: even to day do I declare that I will render double unto thee;

Isaiah 40:31
But those who wait for the Lord 's help find renewed strength; they rise up as if they had eagles' wings, they run without growing weary, they walk without getting tired. NEV

Exodus 21:2-6
"If you buy a Hebrew servant, he is to serve you for six years, but in the seventh year he will go out free without paying anything. If he came in by himself he will go out by himself; if he had a wife when he came in, then his wife will go out with him. If his master gave him a wife, and she bore sons or daughters, the wife and the children will belong to her master, and he will go out by himself. But if the servant should declare, 'I love my master, my wife, and my children; I will not go out free,' then his master must bring him to the judges, and he will bring him to the door or the doorposts, and his master will pierce his ear with an awl, and he shall serve him forever. NEV

ຂດຂດຂດຂດຂດຂດຂດຂດຂດຂດຂດຂດຂດ

I have heard my dad preach his sermon on Prisoners of Hope many times. The message never gets old. I think that it is because we are those prisoners of hope. I can see myself as the servant in Exodus refusing to leave my master and making a covenant to stay with him. Our master is Jesus and when we come to the cross we make a covenant with him. Becoming a living sacrifice and refusing to leave. It is in this moment that we become prisoners of hope. We are no longer slaves to sin but now we are attached by an eternal covenant that gives us faith, hope, peace, love and eternal life. We have become adopted into God's family.

ຂດຂດຂດຂດຂດຂດຂດຂດຂດຂດຂດຂດຂດ

Prayer
Lord help me to remember my covenant with you. When I am sad, when I am stressed, help me to remember I have hope in you. I have your presence, I have your peace. Lord in the business of my day, help me to remember the day I became a prisoner of hope.

ຂດຂດຂດຂດຂດຂດຂດຂດຂດຂດຂດຂດຂດ

Notes

_____

_____

_____

_____

_____

DOG OF BLUE

୫୦୫୦୫୦୫୦୫୦୫୦୫୦୫୦୫୦୫୦୫୦୫୦

Prayer Requests

_____

_____

_____

_____

_____

_____

Day 29

WAITING

Are you listening for the Fathers footsteps
Or the other Shoe to Fall?
We have this expression quite well known to all
"He's waiting, for the other Shoe to Fall"
An accident waiting to happen
Tragedy in anticipation
But our loving Heavenly Father
Wants to walk with us each day
In the garden of your life
Can you hear His footsteps?
Coming your way?
Good times and bad come to one and all
But it's only the sadder times
That many seem to recall
They are constantly waiting
For the other shoe to fall
Let the memories comfort you
Of Love "n" Loyalty
And things that were a Blessing to all
And you'll be Foot Step Waiting

DOG OF BLUE

Instead of Shoe Falling Anticipating
Shake the blues
Put on your shoes
Be ready to answer the Call
Give it a try
You could die
Waiting for the Other Shoe to Fall

꼰꼰꼰꼰꼰꼰꼰꼰꼰꼰꼰꼰꼰꼰꼰

Matthew 10:26-31
Do not be afraid of them, for nothing is hidden that will
not be revealed, and nothing is secret that will not be
made known. What I say to you in the dark, tell in the
light, and what is whispered in your ear, proclaim from
the housetops. Do not be afraid of those who kill the
body but cannot kill the soul. Instead, fear the one
who is able to destroy both soul and body in hell.
Aren't two sparrows sold for a penny? Yet not one of
them falls to the ground apart from your Father's will.
Even all the hairs on your head are numbered. So do
not be afraid; you are more valuable than many
sparrows. NEV

꼰꼰꼰꼰꼰꼰꼰꼰꼰꼰꼰꼰꼰꼰꼰

I love this poem because the phrase "waiting for the other
shoe to drop" has always irritated me. It speaks of fear,
anticipating more "bad things" to happen. Dear friend, don't
wait for the other shoe to drop...wait for God to do

POEMS TO LIVE BY

something great. Why should we spend all of our
emotional energy, waiting for something bad to happen,
when we can be expecting something good to happen?
Don't live in fear of what tomorrow may hold. Live in faith
knowing that you serve a God who loves you and only
wants the best for you. If God knows each time a sparrow
falls or every time you lose one hair on your head, how
much more does he care about you?

ഇഇഇഇഇഇഇഇഇഇഇഇഇഇഇ

Prayer
Lord, I don't want to live in fear. I want to live in faith
knowing that you care about every detail in my life. Teach
me Lord to look for the best and not fear the worst. I trust
you today with all of my plans. Keep my mind stayed in you
and not on the situations that cause me fear.

ഇഇഇഇഇഇഇഇഇഇഇഇഇഇഇ

Notes

_____
_____
_____
_____
_____
_____
_____

ഇഇഇഇഇഇഇഇഇഇഇഇഇഇഇ

DOG OF BLUE

Prayer Requests

_____
_____
_____
_____
_____
_____
_____

Day 30

JESUS STOLE SIN

Stored in the earth deep within
The devil's barrels filled with gin
Squeezed from worldlings
He had tempted to sin
Jesus was brought
A glimpse of him
They eagerly sought
To their horror
They covered their face
Too much light
Was filling the place
They sent Him off to
The wine cellar deep
There they thought
The light would keep
The banquet was about to proceed
Gremlins nibbling
On hors d'oeuvres of
Jealousy and greed

DOG OF BLUE

But while they looked on each
Other in disdain
Jesus was beating them
At their own game
This the finest hour of grace
Jesus stole the sin
And put his blood in its place
And when the blood from the
Bottles was poured
A shriek went up from the grungy hoard
Just one sniff of that living juice
And it made all Hell break loose
To the ends of the earth
They began to scatter
Leaving the devil
To look into the matter
Jesus a thief ?
That's beyond belief
But what happened in that cellar
We really can't tell
One things for sure
The rules have changed
Since the night
The lights went on in Hell

න්‍යඤ්‍යඤ්‍යඤ්‍යඤ්‍යඤ්‍යඤ්‍යඤ්‍යඤ්‍යඤ්‍යඤ්‍යඤ්‍යඤ්‍ය

1 Peter 3:18-19
For Christ once also hath once suffered for sins, the just for the unjust, that He might bring us to God, being put to death in the flesh, but quickened by the Spirit; By which also He went and preached unto the spirits in prison.

જાજાજાજાજાજાજાજાજાજાજાજાજાજાજા

Wow! Jesus changed everything. Imagine the scene in hell. Jesus won the victory for you and me. There is no more death and no more pain for those who accept Jesus. The power of Hell has no authority over us. Jesus saved us and set us free. The blood he shed on the cross beat the devil at his own game. He held our souls captive believing he had won but Jesus paid the price and now we are free. Praise the Lord.

જાજાજાજાજાજાજાજાજાજાજાજાજાજાજા

Prayer
Lord Jesus, I am so grateful for your amazing gift of salvation. I am overwhelmed by your mercy and your grace. That you would give your life for mine is a wonder indeed. Help me to always keep this gift in my mind. As I go about my day help me to be thankful for all you have done for me. Not only did you turn the lights on in Hell but you turned your light on inside of me. Thank you!

જાજાજાજાજાજાજાજાજાજાજાજાજાજાજા

DOG OF BLUE

Notes

_____
_____
_____
_____
_____
_____

ഩഩഩഩഩഩഩഩഩഩഩഩ

Prayer Requests

_____
_____
_____
_____
_____
_____
_____

Day 31

BIRD WORSHIP

Way back at creation
When water from earth was separated
As soon as there was a place for a nest
The bird God created

Why would God create a bird
Before there was a man
There must be a reason
He always has a plan

Back when the world was young
Before Eve to Adam He did bring
God designed a way
To teach Adam how to sing

To humiliate satan,
God did aspire
Seems he had taken off
And with him took heavens choir

DOG OF BLUE

So God created man
With only a canary as his mentor
Infuriating Satan
Knowing Adam could sing better

Now here is an amazing thing
Before there was a DD in Theology
Adam was taught to sing
There was no creed for him to keep

Only simple directions
Of which tree to eat
While the serpent
Was securing his eschatology
The bird was teaching them to worship
With God the obvious priority

Worship is what it's all about
Our destiny to aspire
Just practicing for a place
In the heavenly choir
Makes one wonder
Of which tree does theology
Trace its genealogy

಄಄಄಄಄಄಄಄಄಄಄಄಄಄

Genesis 1:21
And God created whales, and every living creature that moveth, which the waters brought forth abundantly, after their kind, and every winged foul after his kind and God saw that it was good.

ಐಐಐಐಐಐಐಐಐಐಐಐಐಐ

We were created to worship, we were created to sing. Today we hear music everywhere. People love to sing. It is a part of who we humans are. We are singers. Unfortunately many sing of things they know nothing about. There are songs about love, family, freedom, divorce, fear, drugs, hatred, violence and death. Yet there is one song that is above all others and that is the song that comes from deep within a soul when he worships God. God is looking for those who will sing to him. We were created to worship.

One day while I was in the Philippines, a typhoon came. I remember standing close to the doorway watching the storm as it faded away. Suddenly I heard a bird singing. I was amazed that as soon as the storm passed the birds were singing. The storm didn't stop their song. Don't let the storms stop your song. Keep on singing right through the storms.

ಐಐಐಐಐಐಐಐಐಐಐಐಐಐ

DOG OF BLUE

Prayer
Lord today I want to be a worshiper. Help me to sing to
you regardless of my day. Fill me with your spirit so I can
be like the birds who sing. They sing all day long
regardless of the world around them. I want to be like
them. Fill my mouth with singing.

ഇ൚ഇ൚ഇ൚ഇ൚ഇ൚ഇ൚ഇ൚ഇ൚ഇ൚ഇ൚ഇ൚ഇ൚

Notes

_____

_____

_____

_____

_____

_____

ഇ൚ഇ൚ഇ൚ഇ൚ഇ൚ഇ൚ഇ൚ഇ൚ഇ൚ഇ൚ഇ൚ഇ൚

Prayer Requests

_____

_____

_____

_____

_____

_____

COMING SOON

Poems To Live By Volume 2
Any Ol Bush Will Do

OTHER BOOKS BY DEBBY DAVIS

Suddenly
Keepers of Salt
Keepers of Salt Study Guide
The Only Way Out Is In
Peace